PATIENCE

PARENT-TEACHER COLLECTION

by

Carole MacKenthun, R.S.M.
and Paulinus Dwyer, O.P.

illustrated by Vanessa Filkins

D1533654

Cover by Vanessa Filkins

Songs by Helen Friesen and Grace Click

Shining Star Publications, Copyright © 1986
A Division of Good Apple, Inc.

ISBN No. 0-86653-364-8

Standardized Subject Code TA ac

Printing No. 9876543

Shining Star Publications
A Division of Good Apple, Inc.
Box 299
Carthage, IL 62321-0299

Unless otherwise indicated, the King James version of the Bible was used in preparing the activities in this book.

DEDICATION

For Peg, whose life has been guided in a special way by the Providential Designs of God.

INTRODUCTION

" . . . bring forth fruit with patience."   Luke 8:15

Today we live in a quick-paced society of fast-foods, instant information and busy schedules. Because of this, patience is often a rarely exhibited virtue and a difficult one to possess.

Yet, when we pause and reflect, we come to the realization that nothing worthwhile in life is sudden. We wait for the birth of a baby. We wait for flowers to bloom in springtime. We wait for the Lord to reveal Himself to us. Waiting is a part of living.

Growth in patience is essential if each of us is to develop fully as a person. The Spirit of Jesus gently bestows His fruit of patience on all those who wait.

The purpose of this book is to aid parents and educators in teaching children about this neglected virtue of patience. Contained in this book are work sheets, games, songs, puzzles and a prayer service that will motivate children to learn about God's patience, the patience of others and their own patience. These activities can be completed either alone or in a group. A Scriptural passage on patience is listed at the top of each idea, and more references are given in the back of the book for reflection or to embellish the activities.

Shining Star Publications, Copyright © 1986, A division of Good Apple, Inc.

TABLE OF CONTENTS

Shining Star Publications, Copyright © 1986, A division of Good Apple, Inc.

GOD'S PATIENCE

"In your patience possess ye your souls."   Luke 21:19

⎯ WAITING ⎯

I asked for health,
that I might do greater things;
I was given infirmity,
that I might do better things . . . .

I asked for riches,
that I might be happy;
I was given poverty,
that I might be wise . . . .

I asked for power,
that I might have the praise of men;
I was given weakness,
that I might feel the need of God . . . .

I asked for all things,
that I might enjoy life;
I was given life,
that I might enjoy all things . . . .

I got nothing that I asked for—
but I got everything I hoped for.
Almost despite myself,
my unspoken prayers were answered.
I am among all men,
most richly blessed.

Author unknown

The virtue of *Patience* is the willingness to wait for God's help. Sometimes we beg God in prayer for something, but God does not give it to us. He gives us something we need more. Sometimes we do not even know what we need. Patience is waiting for God to show us.

This beautiful poem, written a very long time ago by an unknown author, tells us of God's care.

Use the poem to make a poster. You may use the whole thing or only that part which seems best for you. Then decorate your poster and hang it where you can see it frequently.

"But thou hast fully known my doctrine, manner of life, purpose, faith, longsuffering, charity, patience."

II Timothy 3:10

TV PRESENTATION

God's patience is everlasting. It will never end. No matter how great our misconduct, He loves us infinitely and wants us to come to Him and be happy with Him forever. The Bible shows us God's infinite love in the pleading of Abraham for the inhabitants of Sodom. Jesus also tells us again and again in His many stories of God's patience with sinners.

In the following Scripture references, read about God's patience as shown to Abraham and through stories Christ told the people of Israel. Pick one of these and prepare a TV program based on it.

1. Destruction of Sodom - Genesis 18:22-33
2. Prodigal Son - Luke 15:11-32
3. Lost Sheep - Matthew 18:11-14
            Luke 15:4-7
4. Lost Coin - Luke 15:8-10

A "television set" can be made for the presentation from a fairly large cardboard box. Cut a "screen" in the bottom of the box, and cut off the excess folds from the top. Decorate the box to resemble a television and include knobs, dial, etc.

If the box is large enough, one or two children can poke their heads in the back and present a rendition of the story in the form of a newscast. An alternative is to use puppets for the presentation as a play.

"I know thy works, and thy labour, and thy patience . . . ." Revelation 2:2

FINGER PUPPET PARABLE

Sometimes we find it hard to understand why we should be patient with others who do wrong.

Once the people asked Jesus why God did not punish the wrong-doers. Jesus answered by telling a story. You can find this story in Matthew 13:24-30 and Jesus' explanation of the story in Matthew 13:36-43. Read the story and discuss it with your friends or classmates. Then use it for a puppet play. Use the finger puppets on this page in your play.

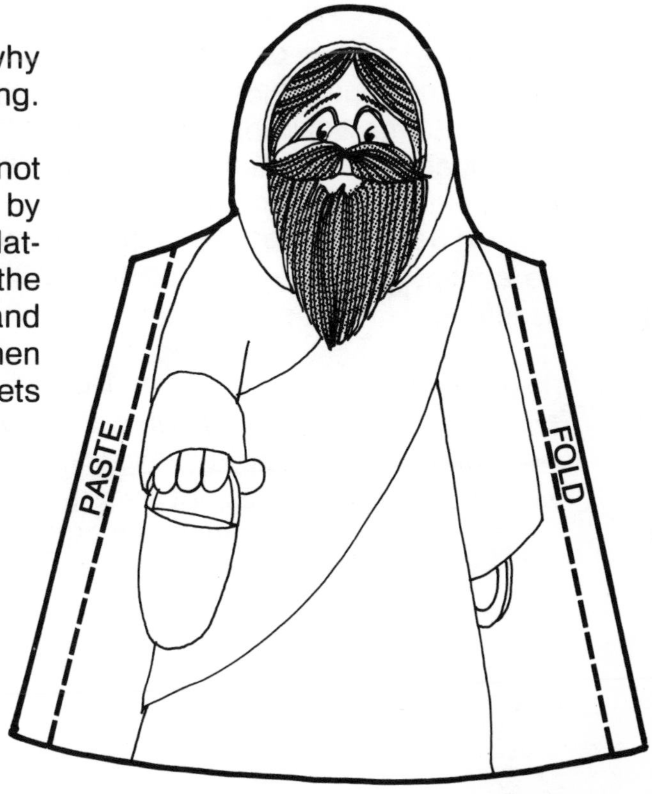

OWNER

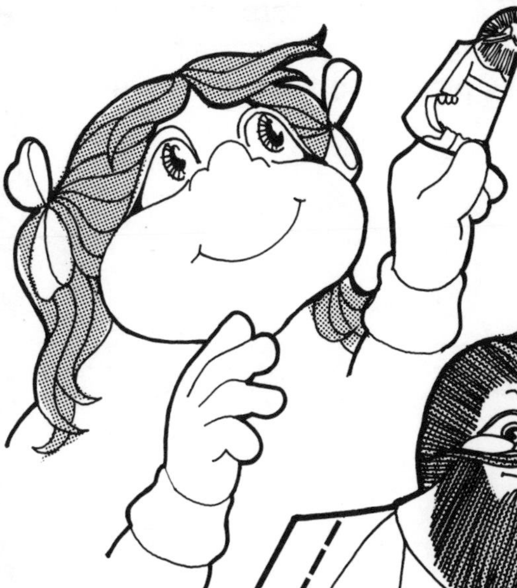

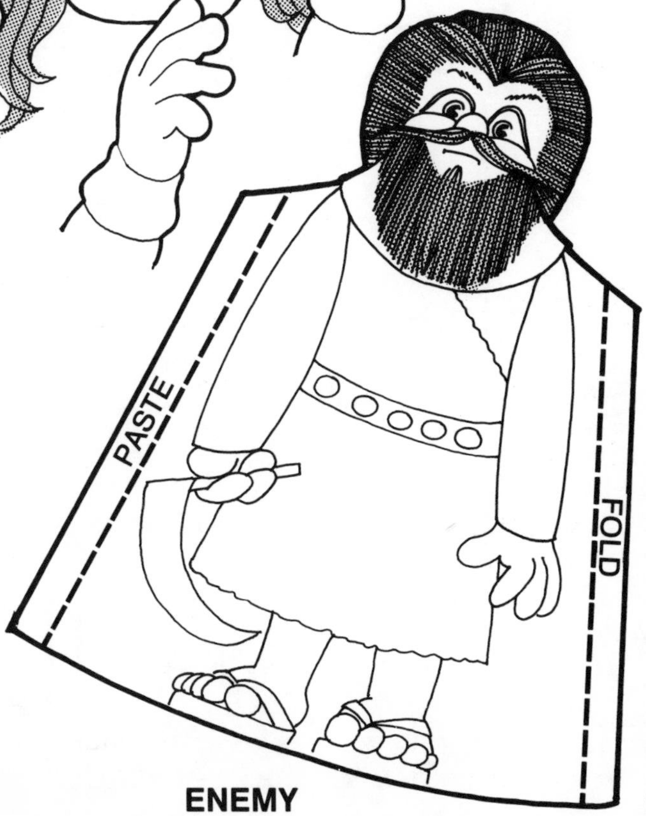

ENEMY

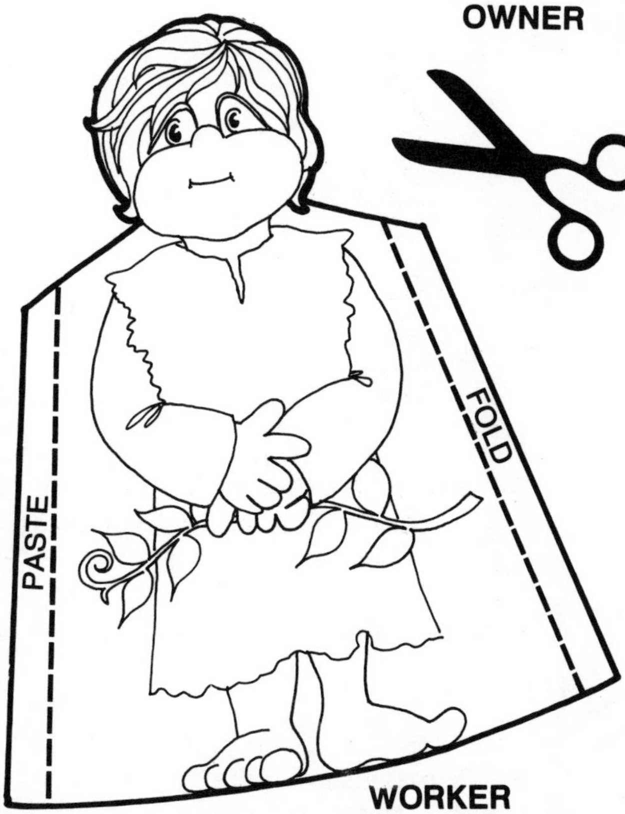

WORKER

"What if God, willing to show his wrath, and to make his power known, endured with much longsuffering the vessels of wrath fitted to destruction . . . ."

MODERN STORY

Perhaps the most difficult person to be patient with is oneself. Once God showed the importance of this when the prophet, Jeremiah, was visiting a shop where the worker was making dishes, water jugs, and other household utensils. Jeremiah noticed that, as the potter worked, if the jug was not exactly right, he would pinch off a piece here and push in a spot there until it was perfect. God showed Jeremiah that this is the way He forms people. It may be painful, but if we accept the suffering patiently, in the end, God makes us into something beautiful.

Read this story in Jeremiah 18:1-6 and Paul's explanation in Romans 9:20-24. Then, in the space below, write the story as though it happened to you in the present time. Perhaps you have visited a seamstress who is making someone's wedding dress. She rips out a seam here and cuts off a bit of lace there until she gets it just right. Or it may be an autobody shop. The mechanic sands the paint or removes a worn belt and throws it away for a new piece. God shapes us in similar ways.

Shining Star Publications, Copyright © 1986, A division of Good Apple, Inc.

PRAYER CELEBRATION

HYMN: "The Children's Friend," page 45

OPENING PRAYER: Heavenly Father, give us the rare gift of patience. Teach us how to wait, how to bear sufferings and how to forgive. Amen.

FIRST READING: Matthew 19:13-15 (An adaptation)
Then one day while Jesus was preaching, the little children tried to come to Him. The disciples wanted them to go away but Jesus said, "Do not forbid the little children to come to Me, for such is the kingdom of heaven." He put His hands on them and blessed them.

PICTURE MEDITATION: Pretend you are one of these children in the picture with Jesus. You wait your turn to speak to Him . . . . Now He looks at you . . . . Tell Him what you want to say to Him . . . . Do you wish to tell Him about a joy . . . a sorrow . . . something that concerns you . . . something that you need . . .? Speak to Him with all your heart . . . . Listen to what He says to you in return . . . . Treasure His words . . . .

PRAYER OF PATIENCE:
Leader: Now let us pray for all those who have shown patience in their lives . . . .
(Spontaneously say aloud those who come to your mind, such as parents, teachers, farmers, etc.)

BLESSING: May the Spirit of Jesus grant to us the gift of perfect patience. Amen.

THE PATIENCE OF OTHERS

" . . . an example of suffering affliction, and of patience."   James 5:10

MESSAGE IN STONE

THE LORD SAID: "THE VISION IS YET FOR A FUTURE TIME. IN THE END IT WILL SPEAK AND NOT LIE."

God appeared to Habakkuk during a very trying period of Jewish history, encouraging the Israelite people to have courage and patience. Then God instructed Habakkuk to write the message He would give upon a stone for the people to see. Part of the message is shown on the stone to the left. Copy the four lines on the blank lines below.

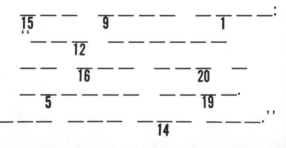

Now figure out the rest of the message. All the letters needed to decode it are above the numbers in the lines you have copied. Copy the numbered letters in the numbered blanks below.

$\overline{15}\ \overline{18}\ \overline{14}\ \overset{U}{\underline{}}\ \overset{G}{\underline{}}\ \overline{18}\ \ \overline{23}\ \overline{15}\ \ \overline{25}\ \overline{18}\ \overline{1}\ \overline{9}\ \overline{9}\ \ \overline{15}\ \overline{1}\ \overline{20}\ \overline{20}\ \overline{16}\ '$

$\overline{23}\ \overline{15}\ \ \overline{21}\ \overline{23}\ \overline{9}\ \overline{9}\ \ \overline{25}\ \overline{5}\ \overline{20}\ \overline{12}\ \overline{9}\ \overline{16}\ \ \overset{C}{\underline{}}\ \overline{14}\ \overline{19}\ \overline{12}\ .$

Habakkuk 2:3
(adaptation)

"Here is the patience of the saints: here are they that keep the commandments of God, and the faith of Jesus."   Revelation 14:12

JOSEPH

Joseph's patience in the face of the many difficulties which came into his life was best shown when he was told by God that Herod meant to kill Jesus and that he (Joseph) should leave for Egypt. Joseph got up immediately and started out. He had to travel for many days through a desert; he didn't know where he could find a house or a job. But he trusted God to show him.

As you find your way through this maze, think how you must trust God when you have problems. Read the story of Joseph in Matthew 2:7-23.

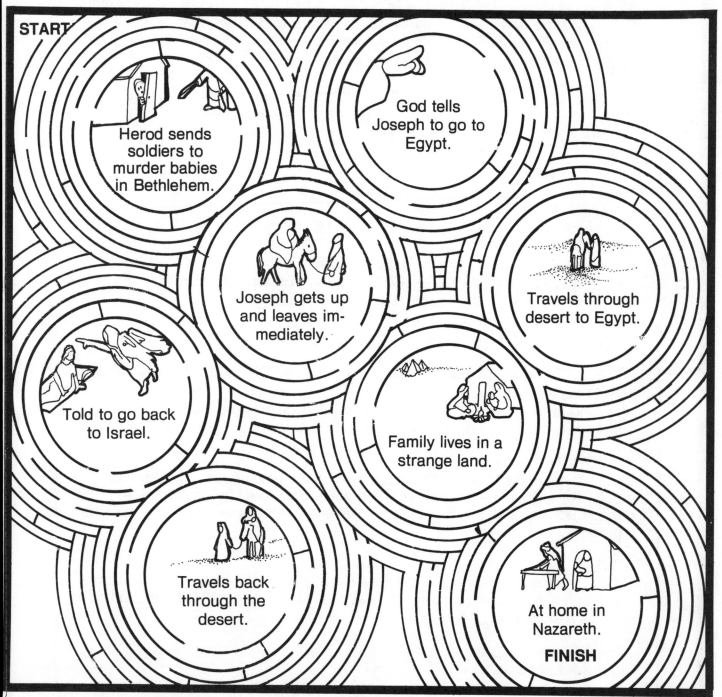

START

Herod sends soldiers to murder babies in Bethlehem.

God tells Joseph to go to Egypt.

Joseph gets up and leaves immediately.

Travels through desert to Egypt.

Told to go back to Israel.

Family lives in a strange land.

Travels back through the desert.

At home in Nazareth.

FINISH

Shining Star Publications, Copyright © 1986, A division of Good Apple, Inc.

"And hast borne, and hast patience, and for my name's sake hast laboured, and hast not fainted."
Revelation 2:3

MAP GAME

INTRODUCTION:
One of the greatest examples of patience of a whole nation during times of hardship was that shown by the Israelites as they passed from Egypt through the desert to the land which God had promised them. Sometimes they complained and were punished for their grumblings, but they never lost faith that they would eventually obtain their goal.

In this activity you will find the location of the places through which the people of God traveled during those forty years on their way to the promised land.

Below are the names of many of these places and references in the Bible where you will find stories of what happened there. You may wish to look these up and study them before playing the game.

1. Rameses	Ex. 12:37 Num. 33:5	11. Midian	Ex. 2:15
2. Succoth	Ex. 13:20 Num. 33:6	12. Sea of Reeds (Red Sea)	Ex. 13:18
3. Kadesh	Deut. 2:14 Num. 33:36	13. Marah 14. Elim	Ex. 15:23 Ex. 15:27 Num. 33:9
4. Moab	Num. 33:48	15. Jerusalem	
5. Jericho	Joshua 5:10	16. Mt. Sinai	Ex. 19:18
6. Dead Sea		17. Red Sea Road	Num. 14:25
7. Meribah	Num. 20:13 Ex. 17:7	18. Edom 19. Wilderness of Shur	Num. 20:18 Ex. 15:22
8. Jordan River	Joshua 3:1	20. Rephidim	Ex. 17:8
9. Wilderness of Paran	Num. 10:12		
10. Wilderness of Sin	Ex. 16:1 Num. 33:12		

MATERIALS:
Map, mounted on heavy paper and laminated or covered with clear plastic; markers; two cubes, one marked from 1 to 6 and one marked from A to F.

DIRECTIONS:
Each player, in turn, tosses the cubes and locates the space indicated (for example, 3 - A would be Rameses). If the player can identify the event that happened there, he/she gets 5 points. * At the end of the game, the player with the highest score wins.

NOTE:
Different translations of the Bible have slightly different spellings of the same name. One may wish to correct spellings to correspond with the edition players are using.

*If more than one place is in the square, player may choose one or tell about both for ten points.

PLACES OF THE BIBLE

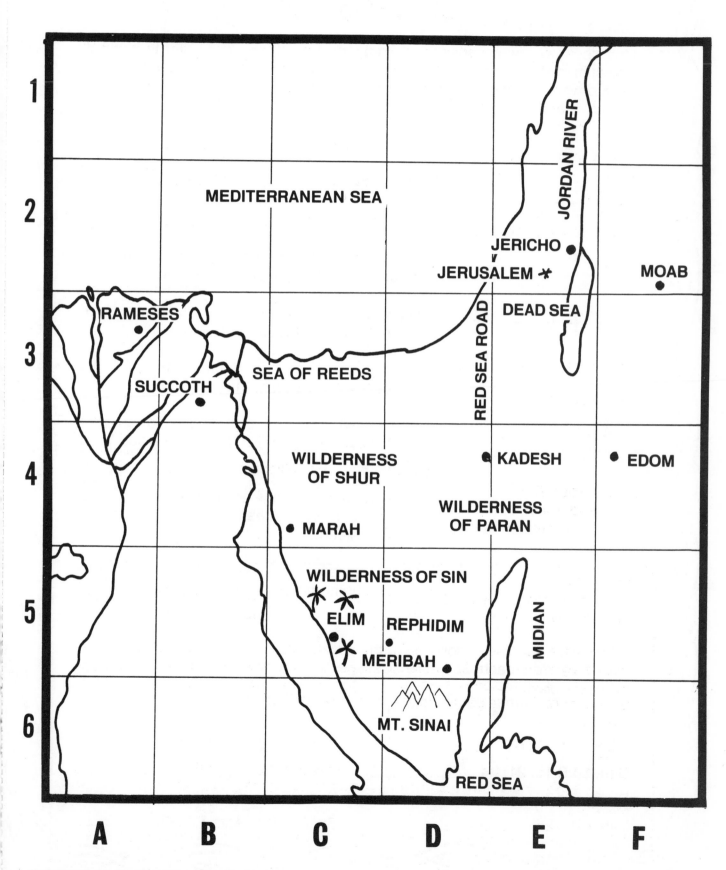

1

2   MEDITERRANEAN SEA

  JERICHO ●

  JERUSALEM ✴   MOAB ●

  RAMESES ●   DEAD SEA

3   SEA OF REEDS

  SUCCOTH ●   RED SEA ROAD

  WILDERNESS   ● KADESH   ● EDOM
  OF SHUR

4   WILDERNESS
  OF PARAN

  ● MARAH

  WILDERNESS OF SIN

5   ELIM   REPHIDIM   MIDIAN

  MERIBAH

  MT. SINAI

6

  RED SEA

A   B   C   D   E   F

"For ye have need of patience, that, after ye have done the will of God, ye might receive the promise." Hebrews 10:36

ACROSTIC

God does not always answer our prayers the way we want Him to answer. Sometimes we wait many years before prayers are answered. Below are some people who waited a long time for answers to their prayers. See if you can identify them.

P _ _ _   God told him that His grace was enough for him.

_ A _ _ _   She waited so long that when the angel told her husband that she would have a child, she laughed right out loud.

_ _ T _   She went to a foreign country with her mother-in-law, trusting what God had for her to do.

_ _ _ _ I _ _   He was patient in his many sufferings even when he was locked up with lions.

_ _ _ E _ _   His patient endurance reunited him with his brothers after many, many years.

_ _ _ N _ _   She waited so long and prayed so fervently in the temple that the priest thought she had been drinking.

_ _ C _ _   He worked for seven years in order to marry the woman he loved, but he was given her sister to marry instead.

_ _ _ E _   He spent many, many years in the desert before God told him the great work he must do.

If you were not able to solve all of the puzzle, look up these references. After you have read each Scripture passage below, write the name on the appropriate blank.

II Cor. 1:1, 12:7-9 _____   Gen. 37:23-32, 45:1-5 _____

Gen. 18:6-15, 21:1-4 _____   I Sam. 1:12-15,19,20 _____

Ruth 1:5-17 _____   Gen. 29:16-30 _____

Dan. 6:11-25 _____   Ex. 2:11-15; Acts 7:20-30 _____

"... be sober, grave, temperate, sound in faith, in charity, in patience.'' Titus 2:2

PATIENT BIBLICAL CHARACTERS

Complete these pictures of biblical men and women who showed great patience. Give a Scriptural reference to prove that these characters show this fruit of the Spirit.

NAME_____

REFERENCE _____

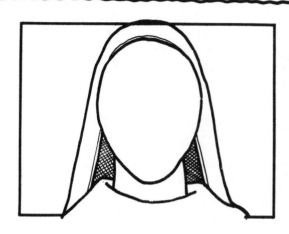

NAME_____

REFERENCE _____

NAME_____

REFERENCE _____

NAME_____

REFERENCE _____

"That ye be not slothful, but followers of them who through faith and patience inherit the promises."

Hebrews 6:12

MESSAGES

Patience is that virtue by which we endure a little frustration (or even, at times, a great deal of frustration) in the expectation that God in His goodness will eventually make all things right. The following messages were sent by the apostles to the early Christians to encourage them in their faith. See if you can translate them; then check the answer key on page 47 to see if you are correct.

Your key to breaking the code is the typewriter keyboard. To decode the messages below, copy the next letter to the left of each code letter as it appears on the typewriter. If the letter is at the far left of the row of keys, begin over again at the far right of the row.

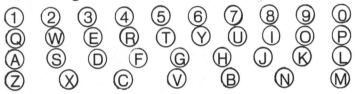

MESSAGE 1

N R D O F R   Y J O D   S F F   Y P   U P I T   G S O Y J   B O T Y I R

_____ ____ ___ __ ____ _____ _____;

S M F   Y P   B O T Y I R   L M P E A R F H R;   S M F   Y P

___ __ _____ _____; ___ __

L M P E A R F H R   Q S Y O R M V R   S M F   Y P   Q S Y O R M V R

_____ _____, _____; ___ __ _____,

H P F A O M R D D.

_____.

MESSAGE 2

N R   Q S Y O R M Y   Y J R T R G P T R   I M Y O A   Y J R   V P Z O M H

__ _____ _____ _____, ___ _____

P G   Y J R   A P T F   N R J P A F   Y J R   G S T Z R T   E S O Y D   G P T

__ ___ ____ _____, ___ _____ _____ ___

Y J R   G T I O Y   P G   Y J R   R S T Y J   N R O M H   Q S Y O R M Y

___ _____ __ ___ _____ _____ _____

I M Y O A   J R   T R V R O B R D   Y J R   R S T A U   S M F   A S Y R T

_____ __ _____ ___ _____ ___ _____

T S O M.

____.

MESSAGE 3

V S D Y   M P Y   S E S U   Y J R T R G P T R   U P I T   V P M G O F R M V R

____ ___ ____, _____, ____ _____

E J O V J   J S D   S   H T R S Y   T R E S T F   G P T   U P I   J S B R

_____ ___ _ _____ _____ ___ ___ ____.

M R R F   P G   Q S Y O R M V R   Y J S Y   S G Y R T   U P I   J S B R

____ __ _____ ____ _____ ___ ____

F P M R   Y J R   E O A A   P G   H P F   U P I   Z S U   T R V R O B R

____ ___ ____ __ ___ ___ ___ _____

Y J R   Q T P Z O D R.

___ _____.

"... let us run with patience the race that is set before us." Hebrews 12:1

EXPRESSING PATIENCE

Ask ten friends to rank in order the ways they show patience to others. Then rank in order the ways that you show patience to others.

1 = most frequent way

5 = least frequent way

NAME	Letting someone go ahead of you in line.	Teaching a younger brother or sister something.	Waiting in line in a store or fast-food place.	Listening while the teacher repeats a lesson to a class-mate.	Repeating what you've said to an elderly neighbor or grand-parent.
1.					
2.					
3.					
4.					
5.					
6.					
7.					
8.					
9.					
10.					
MYSELF					

Compare your chart with the charts of two others. What is the most frequent way of showing patience? What is the least frequent way?

Shining Star Publications, Copyright © 1986, A division of Good Apple, Inc.

"With all lowliness and meekness, with longsuffering, forbearing one another in love."

Ephesians 4:2

A SPECIAL THANK-YOU

Sometimes we make mistakes and need others to be patient with us when we fail. Write a thank-you to someone who was patient with you when you were not your best self. Cut out the message and deliver it to the appropriate person. You may want to color your thank-you note before delivering it.

"But let patience have her perfect work, that ye may be perfect and entire, wanting nothing."

James 1:4

QUALITIES OF PATIENCE

Some people have qualities that make them patient. Name some of these qualities.

QUALITIES OF OTHERS

_____
_____
_____
_____
_____
_____
_____
_____
_____
_____

List those qualities that make you patient. Circle your strongest quality.

MY QUALITIES

_____
_____
_____
_____
_____
_____
_____

Discuss a plan with your parents or teacher that can help make you a more patient child.

"But the fruit of the Spirit is love, joy, peace, longsuffering, gentleness, goodness, faith."

Galatians 5:22

FRUIT OF THE SPIRIT

The object of this activity is to teach and reinforce the fruit of the Spirit. Before the class arrives for the day, write a fruit of the Spirit on the chalkboard and cover it by taping a piece of paper over it. Refer to Galatians 5:22,23.

During the day listen for students responses that demonstrate the special fruit of the Spirit for the day. Make a note of what is said; a check sheet with all the students' names on it will be helpful. At the end of the day, hold class discussion. For example, say to the children: "Did you say anything today that demonstrated 'patience'? Did you hear someone else say something that showed 'patience'? Do you remember when . . . said . . .?"

Before beginning this activity, be sure that the children are familiar with all the fruit of the Spirit. Some discussion on phrases that express each would also be helpful. Often these phrases will overlap and show two or more fruit of the Spirit. Allow plenty of time at the end of the day for long class discussions. Accept everyone's ideas and encourage creative thoughts. Some possible examples follow for your convenience.

KINDNESS:
"I am proud of my perfect spelling paper, but my mother helped me study, so she should get some of the credit."

SELF-CONTROL:
"I am trying to eat less sweets. I had two cavities the last time I saw my dentist."

GENTLENESS:
"Yesterday I found a bird with a broken wing. I put it in a box and I am feeding it until it is strong enough to fly.

PEACE
"Let's not argue."

PATIENCE
"I will wait my turn."

LOVE
"I like you."

FAITH
"I have been praying for you."

JOY
"I am happy."

GOODNESS
"Teacher, may I help you clean the room?"

Some fruit of the Spirit awards are found on the following two pages. You may wish to use these as reinforcements to give to the students. They can also be used to make a mobile or a bulletin board.

FAITH

LOVE

Fruit of the Spirit

JOY

GOODNESS

PATIENCE

PEACE

SELF-CONTROL

KINDNESS

GENTLENESS

I AM PATIENT

"I know thy works, and charity, and service, and faith, and thy patience, and thy works; and the last to be more than the first." Revelation 2:19

NAMES

The letters of your first name can be used to make a PATIENCE PATTERN. Use each letter as the first letter of a patience slogan which will remind you of everyday happenings that you can use to practice the virtue.

Two patterns made by students might read:

C Can let my brother color in my coloring book if he wants to.
I If my friend is crying, I will put my arms around her to comfort her.
N Never answer when I am angry.
D Don't make fun of other children just because they are different.
Y You can play with your toys if someone else wants to watch his/her program on TV.

K Keep my mouth shut when someone scolds me.
E Eat whatever is served without complaining.
V Vow to get up right away when called.
I I will not be angry when the guys tease me.
N Never roughhouse inside the house.

— _____
— _____
— _____
— _____
— _____
— _____
— _____
— _____
— _____
— _____

" . . . the longsuffering of our Lord is salvation; even as our beloved brother Paul also according to the wisdom given unto him hath written unto you."
II Peter 3:15

PATIENCE WITH PARENTS

It is very important for parents and children to be patient with each other. Impatience can be a source of stress for all those concerned.

A. Describe a time when you had to be patient with your parents.

B. Describe a time when your parents had to be patient with you.

C. Write some practical ways for families to be patient with each other.

PERFECT PATIENCE

A. Write some ways that you could be more patient.

1. _____
2. _____
3. _____
4. _____
5. _____
6. _____

B. Circle one way that you would like to start trying NOW.

C. What would you have to do to make this become a reality?

_____
_____
_____
_____

D. Write a personal prescription designed to improve your patience.

℞ NAME_____

Renew 1 2 3 4 times.

(circle one)

"So that we ourselves glory in you in the churches of God for your patience and faith in all your persecutions and tribulations . . . ." II Thessalonians 1:4

DRAW A CARTOON

Use the six cartoon panels below to create a cartoon on patience.

This activity can be done by one person or a group. Stick figures make great cartoon characters.

The first person illustrates a situation of impatience in the first empty panel. The second person takes the situation a step further and illustrates the second panel. Each person adds a new dimension to the cartoon story line. The object is to illustrate how a situation which shows impatience can change to one that shows patience.

1	2
3	4
5	6

Give the cartoon a catchy title.

"Because thou hast kept the word of my patience, I also will keep thee from the hour of temptation, which shall come upon all the world, to try them that dwell upon the earth." Revelation 3:10

ILLUSTRATING PATIENCE

A. Draw yourself being impatient in a true-life situation.

B. Draw yourself being patient in this same situation.

"Truly the signs of an apostle were wrought among you in all patience, in signs, and wonders, and mighty deeds."   II Corinthians 12:12

PATIENT DEEDS

But I say to you, do good to them that hate you and pray for them that persecute you, that you may be children of your Father in heaven.

There are many times during the day when things annoy or do not go the way we would want them to. At these times we can practice patience and grow as children of our Father in heaven.

In each space in the left column below, list something that might happen during your day to annoy you. On the line next to it in the right column, tell how you could act to practice patience. One example is given.

ANNOYANCES

1. I went to turn on the TV and my little brother ran ahead of me and turned on his program.

2. _____

3. _____

4. _____

5. _____

6. _____

7. _____

8. _____

9. _____

10. _____

PATIENT ACTS

1. I did not say anything but went to read my book.

2. _____

3. _____

4. _____

5. _____

6. _____

7. _____

8. _____

9. _____

10. _____

"Remembering without ceasing your work of faith, and labour of love, and patience of hope in our Lord Jesus Christ, in the sight of God and our Father."

I Thessalonians 1:3.

PATIENCE WITH PLANTS

Grow a houseplant. Place your plant in a location where it can be appreciated by yourself and others. Remember to talk to your plant and to give it proper care.

Be patient with your plant and watch it grow! Keep a notebook near your plant and write down any changes you see in it each day.

Write a prayer for your plant. Ask the Lord to make it grow strong and keep it blooming with beauty for all to enjoy!

ALBERT

"Now the God of patience and consolation grant you to be likeminded one toward another according to Christ Jesus." Romans 15:5

HOLDING IN

There are many times during the day that we must hold ourselves in check when others annoy us. If the following incidents happened to you, how could you practice patience? Write your answers in the boxes.

You are watching TV. It is right at the most exciting part. Your mother calls and says: "I'm not going to tell you again to set the table! Do you hear me?" What will you do?

_____
_____
_____
_____

_____
_____
_____
_____

You are in school. The girl across from you hands you a note for her friend. The teacher only sees you with the note and scolds you. What will you do?

Your little brother is playing with your toy. You have told him before that he may not play with it. You are afraid he will break it. What will you do?

_____
_____
_____
_____

_____
_____
_____
_____

It is time to get dressed. Your older sister is still in the bathroom. You want to get to school early to play with your friend. Now you are going to be late. What will you do?

Shining Star Publications, Copyright © 1986, A division of Good Apple, Inc.

"But in all things approving ourselves as the ministers of God, in much patience, in afflictions, in necessities, in distresses."   II Corinthians 6:4

STRIKE TWO

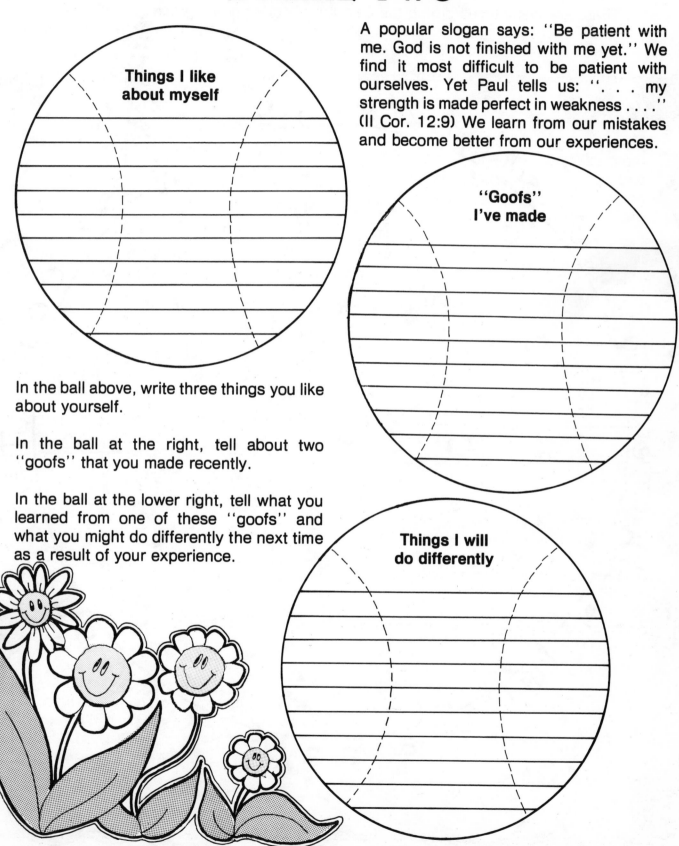

Things I like about myself

A popular slogan says: "Be patient with me. God is not finished with me yet." We find it most difficult to be patient with ourselves. Yet Paul tells us: ". . . my strength is made perfect in weakness . . . ." (II Cor. 12:9) We learn from our mistakes and become better from our experiences.

"Goofs" I've made

In the ball above, write three things you like about yourself.

In the ball at the right, tell about two "goofs" that you made recently.

In the ball at the lower right, tell what you learned from one of these "goofs" and what you might do differently the next time as a result of your experience.

Things I will do differently

"... Here is the patience and the faith of the saints." Revelation 13:10

BRAINSTORMING

Describe a recent situation in which you have experienced impatience. Ask the class to brainstorm solutions for you ....

CELEBRATE PATIENCE

"Strengthened with all might, according to his glorious power, unto all patience and longsuffering with joyfulness."   Colossians 1:11

CINQUAINS

A cinquain (siń-kān) is a form of poetry that has a specific form of five lines and a certain number of syllables in each line. But it is fun to try to write a simplified cinquain using the following scheme:

Line 1—one word; subject (noun)
Line 2—two words; describe the subject
Line 3—three words; action words or a phrase
                about the subject
Line 4—four words; describe feelings about the
                subject
Line 5—one word; refers to the subject

Here is an example of a simplified cinquain:

Patience
Friends, classmates
Hard to achieve
Brings calm and joy
Godlike

Write a cinquain for any two of these words which help you to understand and practice the virtue of patience: understanding, thoughtful, helpful, loyal, concern, mistakes.

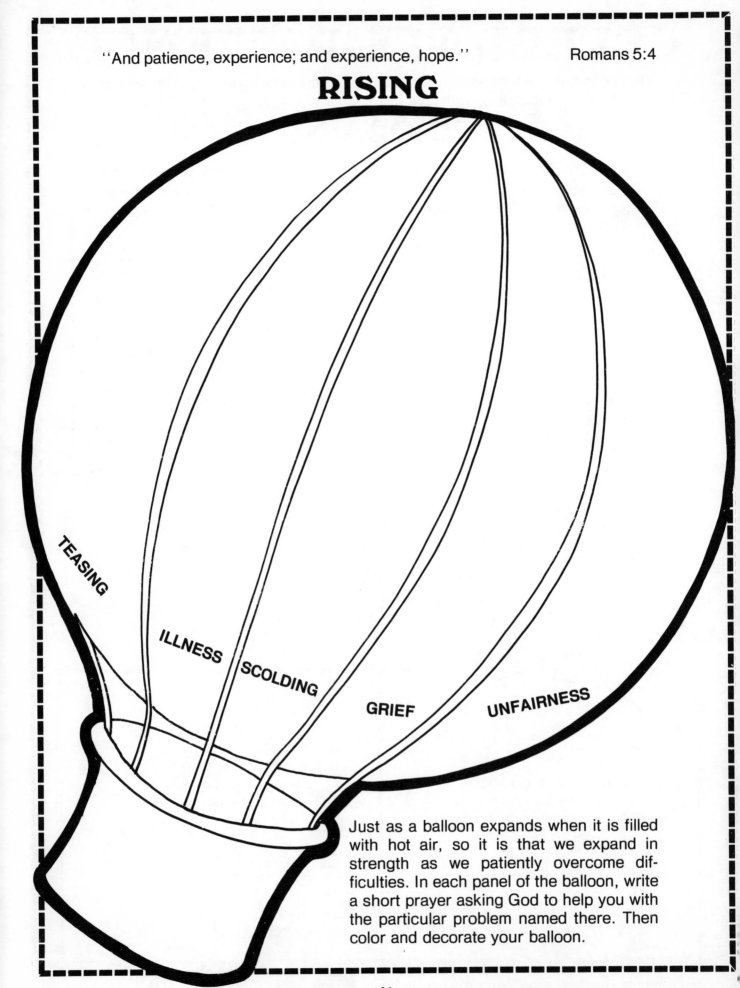

"And patience, experience; and experience, hope." Romans 5:4

RISING

TEASING

ILLNESS

SCOLDING

GRIEF

UNFAIRNESS

Just as a balloon expands when it is filled with hot air, so it is that we expand in strength as we patiently overcome difficulties. In each panel of the balloon, write a short prayer asking God to help you with the particular problem named there. Then color and decorate your balloon.

"Knowing this, that the trying of your faith worketh patience." James 1:3

CROSSWORD PUZZLE

ACROSS

3. Sadness
4. Make grief easier to bear
6. A short, simple song
9. Capacity to endure trouble or pain
11. Relatives
12. Meek
14. Say something unkind
18. Direction toward
19. Close to, within a short distance
20. Happiness
22. First man
24. Put up with, tolerate
25. Our country (abbr.)
27. Makes cars run
28. To encourage, make glad
30. Peaceful, calm
32. To endure with patience
34. Ancient
35. To experience with emotion
36. Blame with angry words

DOWN

1. Satisfied
2. Not up
3. Ill
4. Stop
5. Part of a foot
7. Hello
8. Enraged
10. Bravery
13. Past tense of *tear*
14. Unfairness
15. Northeast (abbr.)
16. South America (abbr.)
17. Annoy by joking
21. Great sadness
23. One of the tribes of ancient Israel
24. Courageous
26. Southeast (abbr.)
29. Aid
31. Hand bars on stairs
33. Not excited

"But if we hope for that we see not, then do we with patience wait for it."

Romans 8:25

MAZE OF PATIENCE

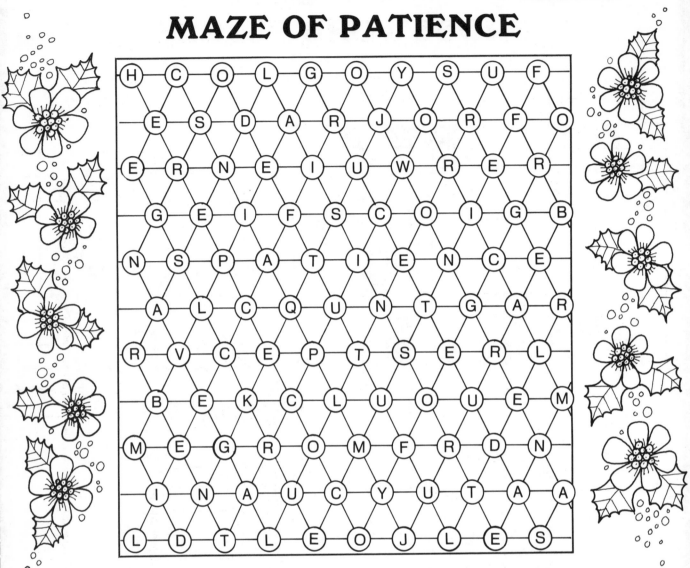

See how many words you can find in this maze. As you look for the words, think how they increase your understanding of patience. Letters may go up, down, forward, backward or even twist. The same letter may be used more than once, but you must follow a line between each letter. Two can play. Keep lists of the words you find. The person who finds the greatest number of words wins.

Words:

accept	anger	bear	brave	cheer	content
comfort	courage	endure	glad	calm	grief
insult	gentle	joyful	just	joy	mild
meek	must	pain	patience	forbear	quiet
sorrow	suffering	serene	scold	tease	won't

PATH OF PATIENCE

One to four players may play this game. They will need markers and a coin. All players' markers are placed in the first space. Each player, in turn, flips a coin. Heads move ahead two spaces and tails move ahead one space. When a player lands on a space, she reads the situation that requires patience and then tells how she could demonstrate patience in this particular situation. The players take turns moving until they have all reached the last space.

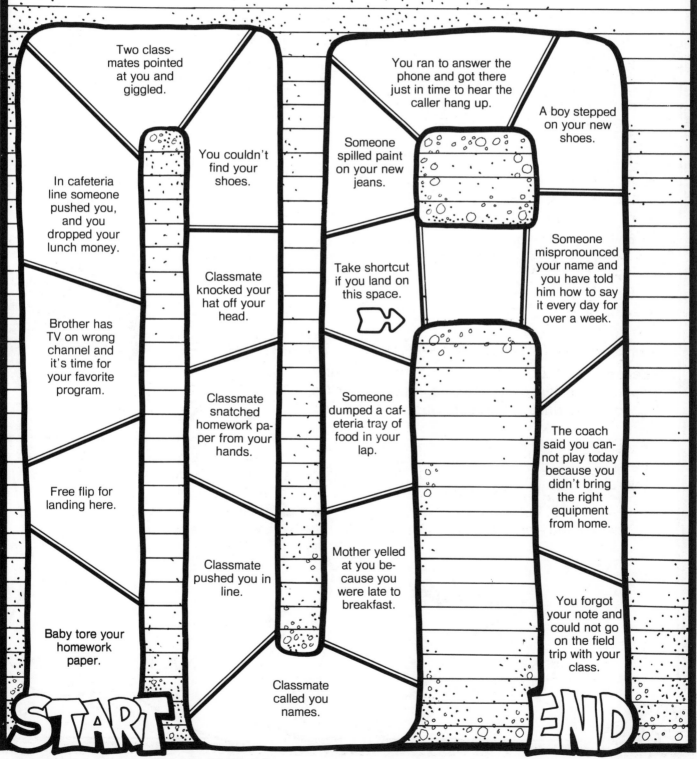

Two classmates pointed at you and giggled.

You ran to answer the phone and got there just in time to hear the caller hang up.

A boy stepped on your new shoes.

You couldn't find your shoes.

Someone spilled paint on your new jeans.

In cafeteria line someone pushed you, and you dropped your lunch money.

Classmate knocked your hat off your head.

Take shortcut if you land on this space.

Someone mispronounced your name and you have told him how to say it every day for over a week.

Brother has TV on wrong channel and it's time for your favorite program.

Classmate snatched homework paper from your hands.

Someone dumped a cafeteria tray of food in your lap.

The coach said you cannot play today because you didn't bring the right equipment from home.

Free flip for landing here.

Classmate pushed you in line.

Mother yelled at you because you were late to breakfast.

Baby tore your homework paper.

Classmate called you names.

You forgot your note and could not go on the field trip with your class.

START

END

"For whatsoever things were written aforetime were written for our learning, that we through patience and comfort of the scriptures might have hope."

Romans 15:4

PATIENT SEARCH

Some of the words we use to describe or tell us about PATIENCE are listed below. See if you can find them in the puzzle. Some of the letters are used more than once. The words may be found across, up, down, or diagonally.

```
J  P  Y  C  O  N  T  I  N  U  E  Q  E
O  E  T  R  O  F  M  O  C  L  K  T  T
B  R  T  A  C  C  E  P  T  J  A  P  O
F  S  S  U  S  E  J  N  N  R  M  M  L
O  E  I  B  L  U  E  Y  E  E  O  Z  E
R  V  S  U  S  G  D  P  T  A  E  M  R
T  E  R  T  H  T  M  A  N  A  L  C  A
I  R  E  C  A  E  P  I  O  A  R  P  T
T  E  P  A  T  I  E  N  C  E  A  S  E
U  R  X  G  E  U  Z  O  S  S  E  G  R
D  U  O  L  N  Q  N  I  S  T  B  O  U
E  D  Y  K  E  T  G  I  O  R  R  O  D
D  N  E  M  R  N  V  S  R  U  O  D  N
B  E  I  O  E  E  F  I  C  H  F  Z  E
M  I  L  D  S  T  R  A  N  Q  U  I  L
```

WORDS:

cease	accept	blue	continue	calm
control	comfort	content	gentle	cross
good	endure	forbear	just	God
led	meek	Job	mild	lie
passive	patience	mend	persevere	moan
persist	resigned	peace	temperate	quiet
tolerate	tranquil	serene	Jesus	tempt
	fortitude	bear		

THE MANUAL ALPHABET

"Put on therefore, as the elect of God, holy and beloved . . . mercies, kindness, humbleness of mind, meekness, longsuffering."   Colossians 3:12

The manual alphabet is a valuable tool for anyone with a serious hearing handicap. Patience, time and effort are needed to learn it. Study the manual alphabet, one line at a time. Practice signing the word *patience*, and then try the other fruit of the Spirit. Can you sign your favorite Bible verse?

A B C D E F G H I

J K L M N O P Q R

S T U V W X Y Z and

1 2 3 4 5 6 7 8 9 10

SIGN LANGUAGE

Now try to learn the sign language for the word *patience*.

PATIENCE

Shining Star Publications, Copyright © 1986, A division of Good Apple, Inc.

"But that on the good ground are they, which in an honest and good heart, having heard the word, keep it, and bring forth fruit with patience." Luke 8:15

MIRROR, MIRROR

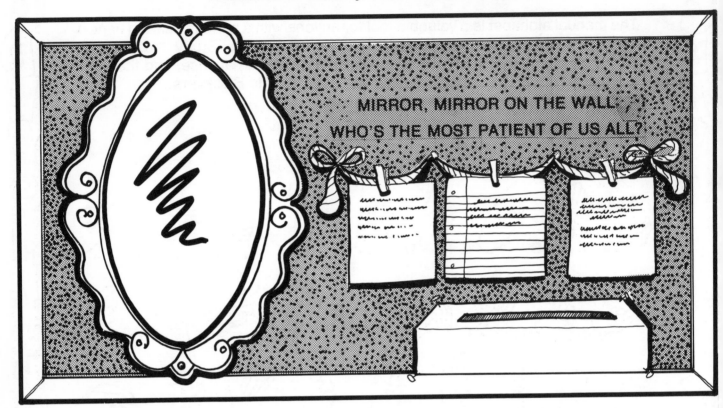

PURPOSE: This bulletin board encourages the children to show patience in their lives.

PROCEDURE:
1. The mirror is made of oaktag covered with aluminum foil.
2. Yarn or string with plastic clothespins is attached to the bulletin board.
3. The ballot box may be a decorated shoe box or a colorful tissue box.
4. Children may write the name of a classmate and how he/she showed patience on a piece of paper and insert it in the ballot box.
5. At the end of the week, the teacher counts the votes to see which three students are the most patient in the class.
6. The students' pictures are hung on the line. Under the pictures the teacher writes the different ways the children have shown patience this week.

VARIATION: Another appropriate title could be:
Mirror, Mirror on the Wall
Who's the Most Patient Bible Character of All?

(Students can submit portraits of Bible characters and compositions explaining their reasons for choosing them.)

"Be patient therefore, brethren, unto the coming of the Lord . . . ." James 5:7

PATIENCE PROJECT

BELL BANNER

Waiting for a special holiday is always difficult. This little project can be placed in your bedroom or classroom to be used to make the time pass quickly.

MATERIALS NEEDED:
Ribbon, approximately 30 inches long and 3 inches wide (any color)
7 bells, at least 1 inch in diameter
Bell poem printed on colored paper

POEM:
Seven days till Christmas
Is the longest time of the year;
Seems that this holiday
Never will appear.

How many more days till Christmas?
It's mighty hard to count.
So this little bell banner
Will tell you the exact amount.

Ring a bell every night
When the sandman casts his spell.
Christmas Day will soon be here
When you reach the final bell.

VARIATION:
Other symbols may be substituted for different holidays. For example:
1. Easter—heads of bunnies
   Add whiskers each night.
2. Thanksgiving—pumpkins
   Put a stem on each night.
3. Halloween—heads of witches
   Add a hat each night.

Seven days till Christmas
Is the longest time of the year;
Seems that this holiday
Never will appear.

How many more days till Christmas?
It's mighty hard to count.
So this little bell banner
Will tell you the exact amount.

Ring a bell every night
When the sandman casts his spell.
Christmas Day will soon be here
When you reach the final bell.

"Which sometime were disobedient, when once the longsuffering of God waited in the days of Noah, while the ark was a-preparing . . . ."   I Peter 3:20

TROPICAL FREEZE RECIPE

INGREDIENTS:
1 can (6 oz.) frozen concentrated orange juice
1 large can (1⅔ cups) undiluted Carnation Evaporated Milk
¼ cup lemon juice
½ cup sugar

PROCEDURE:
1. Take the concentrated orange juice out of the freezer so that it will be softened.

2. Pour Carnation Evaporated Milk into an ice-cube tray; put it into the freezer to chill until there are soft crystals through the milk. That takes about 30 minutes.

3. Pour chilled Carnation into a large bowl. Whip it with an egg beater until stiff—or about 2 minutes.

4. Add lemon juice. Continue whipping until the Carnation is very stiff—or about 2-3 minutes.

5. Mix the sugar and softened concentrated orange juice into the whipped Carnation with a wooden spoon.

6. Put the Tropical Freeze into two small (or 1 large) ice cube trays. Leave it in the freezer for 2-3 hours or overnight.

7. Wait PATIENTLY until it is finished and then ENJOY!

" . . . Christ might show forth all longsuffering, for a pattern to them which should hereafter believe on him to life everlasting." I Timothy 1:16

PATIENCE AWARD
FOR _____,
WHO WAITS PATIENTLY.
PRESENTED BY _____

SONGS TO SING

"Behold, we count them happy which endure. Ye have heard of the patience of Job, and have seen the end of the Lord; that the Lord is very pitiful, and of tender mercy."
James 5:11

SING A SONG OF PATIENCE

Make a list of the biblical characters who were especially patient. Using a familiar tune, write a verse explaining how one of them showed this virtue in his/her life.

For example: (To the tune of "Row, Row, Row Your Boat.")

JOSEPH WAS A PATIENT MAN
WITH HIS OTHER BROTHERS,
EVEN THOUGH THEY ALL SOLD HIM
AS A SLAVE TO OTHERS.

"And his fellowservant fell down at his feet, and besought him, saying, Have patience with me, and I will pay thee all."

Matthew 18:29

THE CHILDREN'S FRIEND
Words and Music
by
Helen Friesen

Jesus was always patient with the little children. Below you will find a simple song about how He feels about children. After you have studied Matthew 19:13-15, Mark 10:13-16 and Luke 18:15-17, write another verse for this song. Make sure you use the right number of syllables so your song can be sung.

Je-sus was the lit-tle chil-dren's friend, And they loved Him, sat up-on His knee; His dis-ci-ples tried to push them out, But Je-sus said, "Let them come to Me."

MY VERSE

PATIENCE BY THE TON
Words and Music
by
Grace Click

To fill the earth with kind-ness, Each one must do his part—

Let's fill the earth with Fruit of the Spirit. Here is one way to start.

Share good-ness by the bush-el, Pa-tience by the ton.

Love, faith and peace We'll share by the truckload, Share these with every-one.

Up! Adds up. (clap-clap) Adds up (clap-clap) Adds up !

Verse 2:
Spread JO-Y by the gal-lon,
Be GENTLE by the score,
Be GOOD and always practice SELF-CONTROL,
Then use all NINE some more.

Let's fill the earth with KINDNESS,
Let's fill the earth's great cup.
Let's fill the earth with FRUIT OF THE SPIR-IT,
Each little bit adds up!
Adds up, (clap, clap) Adds up, (clap-clap) Adds up!

MESSAGE IN STONE p. 10
Though it shall tarry it will surely come.
Habbakuk 2:3

ACROSTIC p. 14
1. Paul
2. Sarah
3. Ruth
4. Daniel
5. Joseph
6. Hannah
7. Jacob
8. Moses

MESSAGES p. 16
MESSAGE 1

Beside this, add to your faith virtue; and to virtue, knowledge; and to knowledge, patience; and to patience, godliness. (II Peter 1:5,6 adaptation)

MESSAGE 2

Be patient therefore, until the coming of the Lord. Behold, the farmer waits for the fruit of the earth, being patient until he receives the early and later rain. (James 5:7 adaptation)

MESSAGE 3

Cast not away, therefore, your confidence which has a great reward. For you have need of patience, that after you have done the will of God, you may receive the promise. (Hebrews 10: 35, 36 adaptation)

CROSSWORD PUZZLE p. 35

ACROSS	DOWN
3. Sorrow	1. Content
4. Comfort	2. Down
6. Chant	3. Sick
9. Patience	4. Cease
11. Kin	5. Toe
12. Gentle	7. Hi
14. Insult	8. Angry
18. To	10. Courage
19. Near	13. Tore
20. Joy	14 Injustice
22. Adam	15. NE
24. Bear	16. S.A.
25. U.S.	17. Tease
27. Gas	21. Grief
28. Cheer	23. Dan
30. Serene	24. Brave
32. Accept	26. SE
34. Old	29. Help
35. Feel	31. Rail
36. Scold	33. Calm

WORD SEARCH p. 38

SCRIPTURAL PASSAGES ON PATIENCE

Matthew	18:26; 18:29
Luke	8:15; 21:19
Romans	5:3; 5:4; 8:25; 15:4; 15:5
II Corinthians	6:4; 12:12
Colossians	1:11
I Thessalonians	1:3
II Thessalonians	1:4
I Timothy	6:11
II Timothy	3:10
Titus	2:2
Hebrews	6:12; 10:36; 12:1
James	1:3; 5:7; 5:10; 5:11
II Peter	1:6
Revelation	1:9; 2:2; 2:3; 2:19; 3:10; 13:10; 14:12